Comptroller's Handbook

A-COC

I0448556

Safety and Soundness

| Capital Adequacy (C) | Asset Quality (A) | Management (M) | Earnings (E) | Liquidity (L) | Sensitivity to Market Risk (S) | Other Activities (O) |

Concentrations of Credit

December 2011

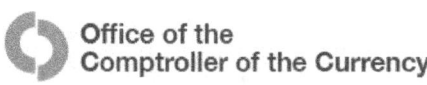

Office of the Comptroller of the Currency

Washington, DC 20219

Concentrations of Credit

Contents

Introduction 1
    Definition 2
    Governance 3
    Pools of Transactions with Similar Characteristics 4
    Identifying Concentrations 6
    Correlation of Pools 9
    Stress Testing 11
    Mitigating Concentration Risk 12
    Management Information Systems 13
    Conclusion 14
Examination Procedures 16
    Quantity of Risk 18
    Quality of Risk Management 20
    Conclusion Procedures 23
Appendix A – Listing of NAICS industries, groups, and sectors. 26
References 29

Concentrations of Credit

The primary source of revenue for most commercial banks and federal savings associations (collectively, banks) is the extension of credit, an activity that concurrently poses a risk to earnings and capital. A bank's credit risk activities, when prudently measured, monitored, and controlled, benefit shareholders, customers, and the communities served. Flawed or shortsighted credit risk management practices, however, are a leading cause of bank failure, which results in investment losses, losses to the insurance fund, business disruption, and reduced service to the community. This booklet helps bankers and examiners to identify, analyze, and establish sound risk management processes for concentrations of credit. Conclusions about concentration risk management will be considered when assigning capital, asset quality, and management component examination ratings.

The accurate identification of a borrower's credit risk and the assignment of a risk rating that describes that risk are at the heart of an effective credit risk management process. But credit risk management does not conclude with the supervision of individual transactions. It also encompasses the management of concentrations, or pools of exposures, whose collective performance has the potential to affect a bank negatively *even if each individual transaction within a pool is soundly underwritten*. When exposures in a pool are sensitive to the same economic, financial, or business development, that sensitivity, if triggered, may cause the sum of the transactions to perform as if it were a single, large exposure.

Excessive concentrations of credit have been key factors in banking crises and failures. Accordingly, this booklet emphasizes the need for boards of directors to ensure that management effectively implements internal processes designed to identify, measure, monitor, and control concentrations of credit. These processes need to consider and incorporate credit exposures that can originate outside of the bank's lending portfolio, including those arising from the bank's investment and trading portfolios and off-balance-sheet transactions. A central lesson learned from past financial crises is that concentrations can accumulate across products, business lines, countries, and legal entities within a banking company. Products containing the same types of risks under different labels and in different booking units, such as structured products and off-balance-sheet funding structures, can mask some exposures and risks.

The focus of this booklet is concentrations of credit risk, but management must also effectively manage other potential risk concentrations. Such concentrations and the associated risks include elevated interest rate risk due to maturity concentrations; liquidity risk due to funding concentrations; or operational risks associated with concentrations of certain lines of business, such as mortgage servicing.[1] Credit risk concentrations, however, are often the most material concentration risk in a bank because lending is the primary activity for most banks.

Definition

Supervisors have long recognized that a large credit risk exposure to a single borrower or family of borrowers, when measured as a percentage of capital, poses a potential threat to a lending institution's safety and soundness, and regulation has imposed a limit on such exposures for that reason.[2] Because of that limitation, individual transactions rarely cause material losses or bank failures. Rather, *pools of individual transactions that may perform _similarly_ because of a common characteristic or common sensitivity to economic, financial, or business developments* have been the primary cause of credit-related distress. If the common characteristic becomes a common source of weakness, loans in the pool could pose considerable risk to earnings and capital. This statement is true *even when each transaction within a pool is soundly underwritten.*

Because a concentration of credit tends to perform like a single large exposure, concentrations have the potential to pose risk to earnings and capital. Depending on how broadly a bank defines its common pools of credit exposures, nearly all banks will have concentrations in their credit portfolios. Historically, concentrations of commercial real estate loans, energy loans, leveraged loans, collateralized debt obligations, counterparty credit, loans to emerging market countries, loan participations, and agricultural loans have played major roles in the failure or material

---

[1] See *Comptroller's Handbook* booklets titled "Interest Rate Risk," "Liquidity," and "Mortgage Banking" for more information on managing these risks.

[2] See 12 USC 84 and 12 CFR 32 for national banks and 12 USC 1464 (u) for special rules applicable to federal savings associations. Federal savings associations also face minimum thresholds and maximum limits on their holdings of some categories of assets. For example, the qualified thrift lender test requires a minimum of 65 percent of portfolio assets be invested in qualified savings association investments. Further, their investments are limited to 20 percent of their assets in commercial loans, with amounts over 10 percent required to be in small business loans; 10 percent of their assets in leases secured by personal property, and 35 percent of their assets in consumer loans. Moreover, federal savings associations are limited to 400 percent of their capital in nonresidential real estate loans. See 12 USC 1467 (a) and 12 USC 1464 (c) for additional detail.

weaknesses of a large number of banks. Other credit concentrations, such as loans secured by first liens on residential real estate, have historically posed fewer problems. However, during the recession of 2007–2009, the banking industry experienced significant losses in these exposures when the national housing market suffered broad declines in home values. This experience indicates that although a concentration has not proven problematic in the past does not mean that it is precluded from becoming a problem in the future. For this reason, bank management needs to monitor and assess the potential risk arising from all of the bank's credit concentrations.

In most instances, concentrated exposures were booked during periods of rapid economic expansion that were typically fueled in part by bank credit and frequently included a weakening of underwriting standards. At many institutions, bank management didn't fully understand how these exposures would perform under stressed economic conditions and therefore did not implement risk mitigation strategies prior to the recent mortgage crisis. During the economic downturn, many correlated exposures deteriorated, resulting in a significant number of banking problems, including failures.

Governance

The Office of the Comptroller of the Currency (OCC) expects banks to implement board-approved policies and procedures appropriate to the size and complexity of their portfolios. These processes, coupled with risk management, loan review and audit oversight, should form an internal governance function that effectively identify, measure, monitor, and control concentration risks to the banks both as legal entities and on a consolidated basis. Such processes should consider the potential impact on earnings and capital and on a bank's operating strategy from known and potential concentrations under stressed market conditions, economic downturns, and periods of general market illiquidity as well as normal market conditions. The results of such analyses should be important considerations in a bank's allowance for loan and lease losses (ALLL) and capital and liquidity planning processes and should be taken into consideration as part of the board's action to approve the institution's risk appetite and limits.

Bank management should provide the institution's board of directors with an analysis of the risk posed by these common pools as well as their potential effect on the bank's asset quality, earnings, capital and liquidity. The OCC expects banks with significant credit concentrations to maintain capital levels substantially above regulatory minimums to help mitigate the risk such concentrations can pose. There also may be cases in which the potential risk to capital is so severe that reduction of the concentration will be the most effective risk mitigation action. On the concentration's page in the report of examination (ROE), examiners should note concentrations or pools of transactions that either pose a challenge to management or present unusual or significant risk to the bank. Examiners should require management to take corrective action when concentration risk management is weak or the quantity of concentration risk is too high.

Pools of Transactions With Similar Characteristics

Historically, the OCC has categorized pools of transactions that may perform similarly (i.e., whose performance is positively correlated) as those that include credit exposures that are

- extended to any one counterparty, borrower, or group of related counterparties or borrowers.
- dependent on the same source of repayment (including guarantors).
- extended to independent borrowers who sell the same manufacturer's product.
- extended to an industry or to economic sectors.[3]
- purchased from a single-source.
- secured by a common debt or equity instrument.
- extended to other financial institutions including but not limited to due from accounts, federal funds sold, investments, net current exposure of derivatives contracts, and direct or indirect loans.
- originated within a geographic area that might also be dominated by one or a few business enterprises.
- owed by a foreign government or related entities.

Industry practitioners and supervisors have further refined this framework over time to include many other sources of concentrations, and typically augment and focus the framework based on the results of stress testing, which may be very revealing of otherwise unidentified concentrations. Although it is impossible to list all of the sources, some of the more meaningful include

---

[3] Usually identified by North American Industry Classification System (NAICS) or Standard Industrial Classification (SIC) codes. See appendix A for the OCC's industry taxonomy and www.census.gov for a complete listing of NAICS and SIC codes. Industry designations in this booklet are drawn from this taxonomy.

- retail products, including, but not limited to, credit cards, home equity lines of credit (HELOC), home equity loans, residential first mortgages, auto loans, boat loans, and manufactured housing loans. In these cases, product features (e.g., target market, purpose, documentation, underwriting criteria, or repayment expectations) constitute the common characteristics and sensitivities of the loans. These pools may be further segmented by
  - whether they are direct or indirect.
  - their vintage, particularly when underwriting was changed or new product features were introduced.
  - their credit scores.
  - their loan-to-value (LTV) ratios, particularly for mortgage-related credit.
- commercial products, including but not limited to leveraged loans and project finance. These pools may be further segmented by industry, geography, and deal sponsor.
- indirect exposure to specific asset types through investments backed by such assets (e.g., collateralized debt obligations) as well as exposure to protection providers guaranteeing the performance of the specific asset type.
- commercial real estate (including construction and development),[4] which may be incorporated into both an industry and a commercial product analysis. Commercial real estate (CRE) merits explicit mention because of its historical volatility and its role in a disproportionate number of bank failures. Banks may view CRE as a product, which would include all transactions secured by commercial real estate. Alternatively, banks may also take an "industry" view, which would include only those transactions where the primary source of repayment is sale or refinancing of commercial real estate or collection of lease/rental payments. A CRE pool may be further segmented by
  - property type.
  - geography.
  - tenant concentrations (listed by name of tenant or by industry).
  - risk rating.
  - credit structure (e.g., fixed versus variable interest rate).
  - debt service coverage.

---

[4] See OCC Bulletin 2006-46, "Concentrations in Commercial Real Estate Lending, Sound Risk Management Practices: Interagency Guidance on CRE Concentration Risk Management" (December 6, 2006), and OTS CEO Memorandum 252, "Office of Thrift Supervision Guidance on Commercial Real Estate (CRE) Concentration Risks" (December 14, 2006).

Concentrations also can arise through a combination of exposures across these broad categories, and bank management should have an understanding of firm-wide risk concentrations resulting from similar exposures across its different business lines. For example, a bank involved in residential mortgage activities should aggregate exposures from its loan portfolio, investment portfolio, derivatives counterparties, conduits, contractual and non-contractual commitments, trading activities, and warehouse pipelines.

It is important to note that, for measuring credit concentrations, management needs to consider off-balance-sheet exposures, including guarantees, liquidity lines, and other commitments. Management should be aware that a single transaction may appear in more than one pool. For example, an individual's open-end revolving account might appear in a retail product category (e.g., credit card or HELOC) as well as in a geographic concentration; a European-based power plant transaction might simultaneously be included in pools defined by project finance, the utilities industry, and a foreign country. Indeed, it is precisely because a single exposure can perform like exposures in other, apparently unrelated pools that concentration measurement is so important. The key risk management objective is to identify pools of transactions that may act like a single, correlated exposure.

Identifying Concentrations

Existing regulatory guidance defines a "concentration" to include direct, indirect, or contingent obligations *exceeding 25 percent of the bank's capital structure.*[5][6] Obligations include the firm-wide aggregate (across all lines of business) of all types of loans and discounts; overdrafts; cash items; securities purchases outright or under resale agreements; sale of federal funds; suspense assets; leases; acceptances; letters of credit; placements; loans endorsed, guaranteed, or subject to repurchase agreements; credit exposure from derivatives transactions; and any other actual or contingent liabilities. The "obligation" (i.e., the amount of exposure) is defined as the committed or outstanding amount, depending on the concentration's characteristics. For example, using outstanding amounts may make more sense for a credit card portfolio, but commitments might better capture the risk of a portfolio of home equity lines of credit or agricultural production loans. For derivative contracts with a counterparty, the credit exposure would be the net current

---

[5] Although "bank's capital" is not defined in the guidance, OCC practice is to use Tier 1 Risk Based Capital + Allowance for Loan and Lease Losses for credit concentration analysis.

[6] See *Comptroller's Handbook* booklet titled "Federal Branches and Agencies Supervision" for guidance on identifying concentrations within federal branches and agencies.

market value of the portfolio of contracts, plus a conservative measure of the potential future exposure of that portfolio.

Traditional concentration measurement has focused on exposure size, and this remains a sound methodology. Banks should recognize as a material concentration any single exposure or group of similar exposures that exceed risk tolerance levels (relative to capital, total assets, or overall risk level) or that have the potential to produce losses large enough to threaten a bank's performance, condition, or reputation, and stress testing is a very useful tool in this regard. Banking law limits the dollar amount of credit extended to a single borrower or family of borrowers to a fixed percentage of capital. Any exposure pool that exceeds 25 percent of capital is, by common definition, a concentration. Not all concentrations measured at this level, however, represent the same level of risk or require the same level of supervision. Management needs to consider the underlying volatility of the performance. Depending on how narrowly or broadly a bank defines a concentration pool, and the risk characteristics of that pool, a larger measured concentration may not necessarily point to a greater threat to earnings and capital. Some pools that meet the regulatory definition of a concentration may warrant relatively little attention, while other much smaller pools may merit a significant amount of scrutiny, ongoing monitoring, and execution of risk mitigation tactics.

For example, a concentration of geographically diversified and soundly underwritten residential first mortgages equal to a large percentage of an institution's capital would generally yield a predictable delinquency and net losses. Although the level of problem assets would not be perfectly stable over time, the portfolio's performance metrics (e.g., past dues and net losses) would likely remain within a reasonably narrow range. On the other hand, the performance of a geographically concentrated pool of construction and development loans heavily focused in a single property type and equal to a much smaller percentage of capital might be relatively unpredictable, with performance metrics falling within a very wide range. During periods of economic stability, the construction and development portfolio might yield a relatively low level of problem assets. But, during periods of stress, those levels might spike and yield losses far in excess of those on the much larger residential first mortgage pool.

Portfolio size and performance volatility are both important variables. The difference in performance metrics between normal economic times and stressful times may vary widely and is a direct measure of risk. Generally, the greater the difference in portfolio metrics between normal and stressful times in conjunction with portfolio size, the greater the risk of that portfolio and the more management attention and capital that it requires. Accordingly, the OCC expects that institutions will allocate their portfolio risk management resources according to the risk that each pool represents rather than solely according to a pool's size. Likewise, thresholds or limits should be set by fully considering the defined pool's risk characteristics. For very broadly defined pools such as CRE, the concentration limits would necessarily be higher than for more narrowly defined sub-segments such as acquisition, development, and construction loans. When banks set higher concentration limits for broadly defined pools—especially where those limits are more than 100 percent of capital—the OCC expects appropriate sub-limits for material groups of segmented exposures.

To focus management attention on portfolios of greater risk (as opposed to using just exposure size), and therefore rank concentration exposures by risk, it is important to estimate potential losses for the pools. Such loss estimates might be based on a combination of historical loss ranges, economic projections, stress testing results, and management judgment. The objective would be to identify loan pools whose individual or collective performance might reasonably exceed internal limits that the bank has established. Such limits might include estimated loan losses that

- are equal to a certain percentage of earnings.
- would reduce the ALLL by a certain percentage.
- are equal to a certain percentage of capital or would move the bank to a lower Prompt Corrective Action Capital classification.
- would force the bank to cut or suspend its dividend.
- would cause a downgrade in the institution's credit rating (e.g., those provided by Moody's Investor Services or Standard & Poor's) that could increase the cost of funds, damage reputation, or limit strategic opportunities.

Lending institutions often combine a size threshold *less than 25 percent of capital* with a credit risk benchmark in order to identify pools that merit heightened scrutiny and monitoring. For example, an institution might choose to define a concentration as *any pool with exposure greater than a certain percentage of capital (e.g., 10 percent, 15 percent, or 20 percent) that exhibits a level of criticized or classified loans that exceeds a certain percentage of the pool's total exposure* (a static measure).

Alternatively, an institution could augment such a definition with one that uses <u>changes</u> in credit risk benchmark levels (dynamic measures), which might provide an earlier warning of increasing risk. One example might be *any pool with exposure greater than a certain percentage of capital exhibiting a level of criticized or classified loans that are growing above a specified rate.*

As with pools, it is difficult to list all of the possible credit risk benchmarks, but some of the more common include

- criticized and classified levels or percentages (or components of them).
- net loss rate.
- nonaccrual or nonperforming rate.
- delinquency or roll rate.
- growth rate in commitments or outstanding amounts.
- risk rating distribution (typically implemented to monitor the proportion of the portfolio in the higher-risk Pass rating grades).
- weighted-average risk grade or credit score.[7]
- weighted-average probability of default.[8]
- expected and unexpected loss.
- required capital allocation (capital intensity).[9]

Correlation of Pools

Transactions that *may perform similarly because of a common characteristic or common sensitivity to economic, financial, or business developments* may be formed into pools, some of which an institution may subsequently designate as concentrations because of their size or risk profile. However,

---

[7] Calculated by multiplying the commitment (or utilized) amount in each risk grade by that risk grade's numeric equivalent, summing the results across all grades and dividing by total commitments (or total utilizations).

[8] While there is no uniformly accepted definition of *probability of default* (PD), the concept generally incorporates recognition that full repayment of principal and interest by a borrower is in doubt. For Basel II purposes, a retail default is defined by product type and delinquency status, and a wholesale default is defined by the likelihood that principal and interest (without considering recourse to collateral) will not be fully repaid, or delinquency status if 90 days or more past due. While the time horizon may theoretically include any period during a credit's contractual life, it is most typically quoted with a 12-month horizon. The calculation is the same as for weighted-average risk grade, except that the PD assigned to each risk grade is substituted for the risk grade's numeric equivalent.

[9] Capital intensity is typically defined as *dollars of economic capital per dollar of committed (or utilized) exposure.*

---

that is not necessarily the end of the concentration identification and risk management process.

Once an institution separates exposures that may behave similarly into pools, the next issue to consider is whether some of those individual pools might behave similarly. The identification of correlated pools of exposure is an extremely important, but difficult, part of managing credit concentration risk. Two pools that do not exhibit strong performance correlation (i.e., similar credit performance metrics) in a benign economic environment may show very strong correlation in a deteriorating environment. For example, many banks assumed that individual pools of residential mortgages, each representing a different geographic area, would not be highly correlated. While this was a reliable assumption during a benign economic environment, the performance of these pools became highly correlated when home prices declined broadly throughout the country. Accordingly, experience and judgment play important roles in helping banks identify pools that might perform similarly in the future.

Banks should review all of their relatively larger and riskier pools—both those designated as concentrations and those not—to determine if there might be an additional level of performance correlation between two or more pools. While the list of all such combinations is potentially long, it is appropriate to focus on the relatively larger or riskier pools to determine if such a correlation exists.

Suppose, for example, that exposure in each of two industry pools, air transportation and hotels, was equal to 15 percent of capital. Although neither might be designated a concentration initially, if there were a downturn in the demand for passenger air service for any reason, the hotel business probably would suffer as well. Both pools would exhibit common performance characteristics and, at 30 percent of capital, may warrant scrutiny.

Depending on the industry groups defined by an institution, there may also be a positive correlation between industries in the same supply chain. An institution may distinctly identify Auto Manufacturing and Fabricated Metal Product Manufacturing within its industry structure. To the extent that borrowers within the Fabricated Metal Product Manufacturing industry sell to auto manufacturers, a downturn in auto sales would negatively affect the performance of both industries.

Stress Testing

Stress testing is an effective tool for identifying correlated pools of loans. Stress testing can be used to quantify the potential impact from different scenarios on those pools of credits. This means altering assumptions about one or more financial or economic variables to determine the potential effects on portfolio performance. These variables might include unemployment rates, interest rates, commodity prices, market rents, vacancy rates or any other variable important to the performance of that type of credit. Bank management should then review the results of those tests to identify potential concentrations and determine potential responses to changes in market conditions that could adversely affect the condition of the banks. While institutions with large and complex portfolios may use sophisticated financial models, institutions with less complex portfolios can use less sophisticated techniques. It is critical to ask the "what if" questions and incorporate the answers into the risk management process. Stress tests can reveal the kinds of events that might present problems.

Lenders may conduct less complex stress tests by evaluating borrower "what ifs," using little technical support. As part of the initial and ongoing credit analysis, a bank can alter assumptions to assess the impact on the borrower. The lender can then aggregate the results at the portfolio and firm-wide levels. At smaller, less complex banks, management often can review a limited number of the largest credits or use statistical techniques to extrapolate results across portfolios. For example, the lender could alter assumptions about office space rental rates. This would permit the bank to determine at what rental rate a project could no longer service its debt. The lender could then aggregate the results across the portfolio to identify what percentage of the portfolio would be vulnerable to a 10 percent decrease in rental rates.

As the bank's knowledge of stress testing grows, it should strive to make the analysis more robust by simultaneously stressing a number of related variables. Banks of all sizes will benefit by supplementing stress testing of significant individual loans with portfolio and firm-wide stress testing.[10] The overall goal is to quantify loss potential and the impact on earnings and capital adequacy.

---

[10] Bank management may want to consider credit modeling software as it becomes more refined and readily available.

Mitigating Concentration Risk

In some cases, a pool of loans may represent a concentration of risk that is difficult to avoid or mitigate. For example, smaller banks may accumulate concentrations because of their more limited geographic markets and the nature of their local economies, and federal savings associations are required to hold a portion of their portfolios in certain asset categories.[11] Larger banks may develop concentrations through mergers, or concentrations may develop as the result of implementing a strategic plan. In any case, a bank must decide whether mitigation is desirable for a particular pool of loans. *At some point, a credit concentration can become so large that, if the common factor influencing the pool deteriorates sufficiently, even a portfolio of well underwritten loans can suffer losses that can deplete a bank's capital.* This possibility underscores why the control and management of concentration risk is so important.

There are many useful strategies for managing concentration risk. Some are incremental, such as reducing risk over a relatively long horizon, while others have a more immediate impact. These strategies include

- modifying underwriting standards to increase exposure to higher quality transactions or to diminish exposure to weaker borrowers. Concurrently, management can increase the level of credit supervision while executing exit strategies from lower-quality relationships (e.g., increasing pricing or tightening terms and conditions).
- expanding the portfolio by booking transactions that are not likely to perform in a similar manner with the existing portfolio. For example, a decline in the price of natural gas might affect borrowers in the Oil and Gas production industry negatively but would have the opposite effect on borrowers in the Chemical Manufacturing industry. Similarly, an increase in the price of steel might boost the prospects of many companies in the Primary Metal Manufacturing industry while pressuring those in Fabricated Metal Product Manufacturing (if the ability to pass through the price increase were constrained). Additionally, there are well-known linkages between industry performance and the stage of the economic cycle (e.g., the relatively strong performance of consumer staples in a weak economic environment).
- altering exposure limits or credit risk benchmarks, such as adjusting limits on commitment or outstanding amounts, or tightening constraints on

---

[11] See 12 USC 1467 (a).

special mention, substandard, doubtful, or nonperforming levels.

- obtaining insurance or guarantees (e.g., from the Export-Import Bank of the United States, the Farm Service Agency, the Commodity Credit Corporation, the Federal Housing Administration, or the U.S. Small Business Administration).
- selling loan participations, or whole-loan sales on a non-recourse basis, to reduce exposures.
- holding additional capital to compensate for the additional risk that may be associated with a concentration exposure.
- buying credit derivative protection (e.g., default or total return swaps on individual transactions or a pool).

Management Information Systems

Procedures should be in place to ensure accurate reporting of concentrations. These reports should support an active and timely dialog with the board of directors and senior management regarding concentration exposures. The ability to accurately identify pools of transactions with similar characteristics and to associate them with various risk metrics on a timely basis depends on the quality and scope of an institution's management information systems (MIS).

The accurate and timely capture of data is of paramount importance and is a requirement of any MIS, regardless of the complexity of an institution's portfolio. A management information system is of little use if there are significant deficiencies in data quality or if data capture is performed with a material time lag. Such a system may provide a false sense of security, while simultaneously directing attention to lower risk pools. An institution should establish clear lines of responsibility for data quality. While different MIS structures may be equally effective, holding officers closer to the customer accountable for data quality generally yields superior results.

While data quality is the foundation of any MIS, the scope of data elements captured should be proportional to the portfolio's diversity and risk profile. Smaller institutions with geographically concentrated portfolios spread across few products likely will have larger but fewer concentrations and should focus data capture on those products. The MIS of larger, more complex, and globally diversified institutions will necessarily capture a more extensive set of elements across more products.

The OCC expects that an institution's MIS and reporting will be accurate and timely and that its scope will be commensurate with the portfolio's diversity and risk profile. The OCC also expects that an institution's loan review, credit administration, or audit department will periodically review MIS credit data and reports to ensure that the quality, scope, and timeliness are adequate.

Conclusion

All banks have credit concentrations. In some cases, this is by choice as the institution seeks to develop expertise in a particular segment. In other cases, it may be the result of mergers or acquisitions. Alternatively, credit concentrations may be unavoidable due to a lender's limited geographic footprint combined with its market's dependence on a relatively few employers or industries. Whatever the reason, it is incumbent on management and the board of directors to ensure that the bank has an effective process in place to identify, measure, monitor, and control concentration risk. The board of directors also needs to ensure that the bank maintains adequate capital relative to concentration risks.

Although each individual transaction within a concentration may be prudently underwritten, collectively the transactions are sensitive to the same economic, financial, or business development events. If something triggers a negative development, the risk is that the sum of the transactions may perform as if it were a single, large exposure.

The size of a concentration, however, does not necessarily determine the risk. Different pools of the same size may represent very different levels of risk. Although 25 percent of capital remains the threshold for capturing concentrations for regulatory purposes, the OCC expects that institutions will build their concentration management process *based on the risk that a pool of loans represents*. The extent of risk mitigation undertaken by each bank should relate to the level of risk posed by the particular credit concentration.

Identifying, measuring, and appropriately mitigating concentration risk is ultimately dependent on the accurate and timely receipt and analysis of data. The absence of a sufficiently robust set of data elements will hinder an institution's ability to identify and monitor concentration risk, regardless of the data's accuracy and timeliness. Similarly, a comprehensive data set is of little use if inaccurate, untimely, or unexamined. The OCC expects that each bank's concentration risk management systems and MIS will be accurate and timely, and that the scope of the data elements collected and analyzed will be proportional to the size and complexity of the bank's portfolio. Examiners should note pools that pose a challenge to management or that present unusual or significant risk to the bank in the ROE. When concentration risk management is weak, examiners should require management to take corrective action.

Examination Procedures

General Procedures

These procedures are intended to assist examiners in determining the adequacy of a bank's credit concentration management process and should be used in conjunction with the more general procedures contained in the "Loan Portfolio Management" booklet. Examiners only need to perform those procedures that are relevant to the scope of the exam as determined by the objective below. This assessment should consider work performed by internal and external auditors and by other examiners on related examinations (e.g., management information systems or the risk rating process).

The examiner conducting the credit concentration examination should work closely with the loan portfolio management (LPM) examiner to identify mutual areas of concern and to maximize examination efficiencies. Much of the information required to perform these procedures will be available from the LPM examiner. Only those concentrations that pose a challenge to management or present unusual or significant risk to the bank should be included in comments on risk management and asset quality.

Objective: To determine the scope of the examination of the bank's credit concentration management process and identify examination activities necessary to meet the needs of the supervisory strategy for the bank.

1. Review the following documents for previously identified problems that require follow-up:

   • Supervisory strategy
   • Examiner-in-Charge's (EIC) scope memorandum
   • Previous reports of examination and work papers
   • Internal and external audit reports and work papers
   • Bank management's responses to previous examinations and audits

2. Obtain the results of such reports as the Uniform Bank Performance Reports (UBPR) and Bank Expert (BERT). To the extent that the call report categories constitute concentrations, identify any trends (e.g., growth, delinquency, nonperforming, or loss) or changes in credit concentrations evident in those reports since the last examination.

3. Obtain and review the bank's

    - credit concentration management policies and procedures.
    - portfolio strategies and risk tolerance parameters.
    - list of data elements captured by MIS for concentration reporting.
    - schedule of concentrations identified by the institution.
    - credit concentration limits and exposure and exception reports.
    - credit concentration reports submitted to senior management or the board of directors.
    - capital planning and stress testing policies, procedures, and results.

4. In discussions with bank management, determine if there have been any significant changes in

    - credit concentration management policies and procedures.
    - control systems, including MIS.
    - credit concentration levels.
    - portfolio strategies.
    - risk tolerance parameters, including changes in credit concentration limits and exception levels.
    - the level of delinquencies, criticized or classified loans, nonperforming loans, or losses in any credit concentration.
    - capital planning and stress testing policies and procedures.

5. Based on an analysis of data provided in the previous steps, as well as input from the examiner assigned LPM and the EIC, determine the examination's scope and objectives.

Quantity of Risk

Conclusion: The quantity of risk is (low, moderate, or high).

Objective: To assess the level of concentration risk associated with the bank's credit portfolio.

1. Analyze the level of risk of each of the bank's credit concentrations. Consider in your analysis the size of the exposure and the concentration's credit quality indicators, including the amount and volatility of and trend in

    - delinquencies.
    - criticized and classified loans.
    - nonaccrual or nonperforming loans.
    - losses.
    - other credit quality metrics used by the bank (e.g., weighted-average risk grade or weighted-average probability of default).
    - Underwriting standards.
    - Exceptions to policy.

2. Determine the risk implications of the following:

    - Significant growth in the size of a credit concentration's exposure, including whether such growth might be masking deterioration in credit quality indicators.
    - Material changes in policies, procedures, or underwriting standards.

3. Review and discuss with management any internally prepared assessments of credit concentration risk (e.g., industry evaluations).

4. Review the local, regional, and national economic trends and outlook, and assess their impact on the bank's credit concentrations.

5. Review the bank's business and strategic plans and evaluate how their implementation may affect the level of risk posed by any credit concentration.

6. Review and discuss with management the results from applicable stress testing and capital planning assessments.

---

7. Evaluate the impact of mitigation strategies on the quantity of risk (e.g., limits, loan sales, or credit derivatives). Consider the objectives of these programs and management's experience with these tools.

8. Give special attention to asset classes with more volatility in performance (e.g., commercial real estate construction, project finance, and leveraged lending).

9. Based on these reviews and findings, assess whether the bank has adequate capital to support the risk posed by its credit concentrations.

Quality of Risk Management

Conclusion: The quality of risk management is (strong, satisfactory, or weak).

Policy

Objective: To determine whether the board has adopted effective policies that are consistent with safe and sound banking practices and appropriate to the size, nature, and scope of the bank's credit concentrations.

1. Evaluate the relevant policies to determine whether they provide appropriate guidance for identifying and managing the bank's credit concentrations. Consider whether the bank has

   - established a tolerance for risk. This may be shown as a percentage of capital or expressed in terms of risk, not simply size (e.g., risk of dollar loss, or risk to earnings or capital).
   - developed a firm-wide framework for identifying credit concentrations across business lines, including consideration of distinct groups of loans whose credit performance may be correlated.
   - established a process for using stress testing to identify potential credit concentrations and to use stress testing to evaluate the potential impact of adverse scenarios on credit concentrations on the bank's capital and liquidity and for reporting those results to senior management and the board of directors.
   - identified roles and responsibilities associated with identifying and managing credit concentrations, particularly those that may cross business lines or otherwise not be under common management.
   - defined the process for setting credit concentration limits and for approving changes and exceptions thereto.

2. Determine whether credit concentration limits are well defined and reasonable. Consider the way that limits are measured and the use of sub-limits for different types and tenors of exposure within a credit concentration (e.g., property types and geography within CRE).

---

3. Verify that the board of directors periodically reviews and approves the bank's credit concentration policies, including relevant limits or strategies on significant credit concentrations.

Processes

Objective: To determine whether the bank has processes in place to provide accurate and timely assessments of concentration risk associated with its credit activities.

1. Evaluate how policies, procedures, and plans affecting credit concentrations are communicated. Consider whether management has clearly communicated objectives and risk limits for credit concentrations to the board of directors and affected staff and whether the board has approved them.

2. In light of the scope and complexity of the bank's portfolio, evaluate the adequacy of the bank's process for analyzing credit concentrations. Consider the following:

   • Does the bank assess the level of risk associated with each concentration?
   • Does the bank's risk assessment aggregate exposures firm-wide and across lines of business?
   • Are the results of the bank's risk assessments, including those from stress testing, appropriately incorporated into the bank's overall capital planning process?
   • Do the bank's conclusions concerning credit concentrations appear reasonable in light of information available from other sources?
   • Is the bank's capital level adequate to support the level and types of credit concentration exposures?
   • Is a formal analysis of higher-risk credit concentrations conducted periodically, and does the bank have an effective system for monitoring developments in the interim?
   • Is the bank's analysis adequately documented and are its credit risk conclusions communicated in a way that provides decision makers with a reasonable basis for strategy development?
   • Are the resources devoted to the analysis of credit concentration, including the number and expertise of staff members, considered adequate?

Personnel

Objective: To determine management's ability to supervise its credit
concentrations in a safe and sound manner.

1. Given the scope and complexity of the institution's portfolio, assess the appropriateness of the credit concentration management structure and the experience of designated personnel. Consider the following:

   - Evaluate whether the expertise, training, and number of staff members assigned to manage credit concentrations is adequate.
   - Evaluate whether reporting lines encourage open communication and limit the chances of conflicts of interest.
   - Evaluate the level of staff turnover and its effect on credit concentration management.

2. Through discussions with management, ascertain the adequacy of written policies for managing credit concentrations and management's knowledge thereof.

3. Ascertain the adequacy of management's practices and capabilities for managing credit concentrations including timely responses to a changing environment.

4. Assess the performance management and compensation programs for staff members managing credit concentrations. Consider whether these programs measure and reward behavior that supports the bank's strategic objectives and risk tolerance limits.

If the bank offers incentive compensation programs, ensure that they are consistent with OCC Bulletin 2010-24, "Interagency Guidance on Sound Incentive Compensation Policies," including compliance with its three key principles: (1) Provide employees with incentives that appropriately balance risk and reward; (2) Be compatible with effective controls and risk management; and (3) Be supported by strong corporate governance, including active and effective oversight by the organization's board of directors.

Control Systems

Objective: To determine whether the bank has systems in place to provide accurate and timely assessments of concentration risk associated with its credit activities.

1. Determine whether management information systems provide timely, accurate, and useful information to evaluate risk levels and trends in the bank's credit concentrations. Consider the following:

   • Are all material credit risk exposures across all lines of business captured (e.g., loans, leases, overdrafts, counterparties, securities, or off-balance-sheet transactions)?
   • Is the breadth of the data elements collected adequate given the scope and complexity of the portfolio?
   • To who are MIS reports distributed and how timely are these reports?

2. Determine how compliance with credit concentration limits is monitored and reported to senior management and the board of directors.

3. Assess the level of review for credit concentrations nearing their credit risk limits. Is there sufficient reporting to senior management and is oversight heightened?

4. Evaluate the adequacy of the system for monitoring current conditions in higher-risk credit concentrations. Consider the types of internal and external resources used.

Conclusion Procedures

Objective: To determine overall conclusions and communicate findings regarding the quantity of risk and management's ability to identify, measure, monitor, and control credit concentration risk. Examiners should consider these conclusions as part of their overall assessment of the capital, asset quality, and management rating for the institution.

1. Prepare a summary memorandum to the LPM examiner or EIC regarding the quantity and direction of credit concentration risk and the adequacy of the bank's process for managing credit concentrations. Consider the following:

- Quality of the bank's process for managing credit concentration, including the adequacy of policies and procedures.
- Asset quality of concentrations.
- Appropriateness of strategic and business plans in light of their impact on credit concentration risks.
- Responsiveness of strategic and business plans to stress test results that identify credit concentrations or material affects from adverse economic scenarios.
- Accuracy and timeliness of management information systems and the breadth of data captured relative to the scope and complexity of the portfolio.
- Quality of staffing, and management's capability to manage concentrations.
- Recommended corrective action for deficient policies, procedures, practices, or other concerns.
- Adequacy of adherence to policies and credit concentration limits.
- Adequacy of loan review or audit functions.
- Other matters of significance.

2. For any issues of concern identified when performing the concentrations of credit procedures, determine their impact on the bank's aggregate credit risk and its direction.

3. Discuss examination findings and conclusions with the EIC, including a list of those concentrations (or pools) posing a challenge to management or presenting unusual or significant risk to the bank, that should be included in the report of examination. If necessary, compose a Matters Requiring Attention (MRA) memorandum for the credit concentration examination. MRAs should cover practices that

- deviate from sound, fundamental principles and are likely to result in financial deterioration or increased risk if not addressed.
- result in substantive noncompliance with laws or regulations.

MRAs should

- describe the MRA;
- identify contributing factors or the root cause(s) of the MRA;
- describe likely consequences or effects on the bank from inaction;
- record management's commitment to corrective action; and

- include the time frame and the person(s) responsible for corrective action.

4. Discuss findings with bank management, including conclusions about credit concentration risks. If necessary, obtain commitment for corrective action.

5. Write a memorandum specifically setting out what the OCC should do in the future to effectively supervise the management of credit concentrations in the bank, including time periods, staffing, and workdays required.

6. Update the OCC's electronic information system and any applicable report of examination schedules or tables.

7. Update the examination work papers in accordance with OCC guidance.

Concentrations of Credit

The OCC uses an industry taxonomy that assigns Standard Industrial Classification (SIC) and North American Industry Classification System (NAICS) codes to 94 industries, which are further sorted into 25 groups and eight sectors. The structure as of June 2011 is shown below.[12]

Sector	Group	Industry
Commodities	Agribusiness	Animal Production
Commodities	Agribusiness	Crop Production
Commodities	Agribusiness	Forestry and Logging
Commodities	Agribusiness	Miscellaneous Agribusiness
Commodities	Materials & Commodities Exc. Energy	Chemical Manufacturing
Commodities	Materials & Commodities Exc. Energy	Mining (Except Oil & Gas & Coal)
Commodities	Materials & Commodities Exc. Energy	Nonmetallic Mineral Product Manufacturing
Commodities	Materials & Commodities Exc. Energy	Paper Manufacturing
Commodities	Materials & Commodities Exc. Energy	Plastics and Rubber Products Manufacturing
Commodities	Materials & Commodities Exc. Energy	Primary Metal Manufacturing
Commodities	Materials & Commodities Exc. Energy	Wood Product Manufacturing
Commodities	Oil & Gas & Coal	Fuel Distributors
Commodities	Oil & Gas & Coal	Oil & Gas & Coal Extraction
Commodities	Oil & Gas & Coal	Petroleum and Coal Products Manufacturing
Commodities	Utilities	Pipeline Transportation
Commodities	Utilities	Utilities
Distribution	Food & Drug Stores	Food and Beverage Stores
Distribution	Food & Drug Stores	Health and Personal Care Stores
Distribution	Retail Stores Exc. Food & Drug	Building Material and Garden Equip. and Supplies Dealers
Distribution	Retail Stores Exc. Food & Drug	Clothing and Clothing Accessories Stores
Distribution	Retail Stores Exc. Food & Drug	Electronics and Appliance Stores
Distribution	Retail Stores Exc. Food & Drug	Furniture and Home Furnishings Stores
Distribution	Retail Stores Exc. Food & Drug	General Merchandise Stores
Distribution	Retail Stores Exc. Food & Drug	Miscellaneous Store Retailers
Distribution	Retail Stores Exc. Food & Drug	Nonstore Retailers
Distribution	Retail Stores Exc. Food & Drug	Sporting Goods, Hobby, Book, and Music Stores
Distribution	Wholesale Distribution	Merchant Wholesalers, Durable Goods
Distribution	Wholesale Distribution	Merchant Wholesalers, Nondurable Goods
Distribution	Wholesale Distribution	Wholesale Electronic Markets and Agents and Brokers
Financial	Banks	Banks
Financial	Finance & Insurance	Credit Intermediation and Related Activities
Financial	Finance & Insurance	Funds, Trusts, and Other Financial Vehicles
Financial	Finance & Insurance	Insurance Carriers and Related Activities
Financial	Finance & Insurance	Miscellaneous Financial

---

[12] See www.census.gov for a complete list of SIC and NAICS codes.

Sector	Group	Industry
Financial	Finance & Insurance	Rental and Leasing Services
Financial	Finance & Insurance	Securities, Commodity Contracts, and Other Financial Investments and Related Activities
Government	Government & Education	Educational Services
Government	Government & Education	Government
Manufacturers	Apparel & Textiles Manufacturing	Apparel Manufacturing
Manufacturers	Apparel & Textiles Manufacturing	Leather and Allied Product Manufacturing
Manufacturers	Apparel & Textiles Manufacturing	Textile Mills
Manufacturers	Auto-Related	Auto Manufacturing
Manufacturers	Auto-Related	Motor Vehicle and Parts Dealers
Manufacturers	Durables Manufacturing Exc. Auto	Computer and Electronic Product Manufacturing
Manufacturers	Durables Manufacturing Exc. Auto	Electrical Equip., Appliance, and Component Manufacturing
Manufacturers	Durables Manufacturing Exc. Auto	Fabricated Metal Product Manufacturing
Manufacturers	Durables Manufacturing Exc. Auto	Furniture and Related Product Manufacturing
Manufacturers	Durables Manufacturing Exc. Auto	Machinery Manufacturing
Manufacturers	Durables Manufacturing Exc. Auto	Miscellaneous Manufacturing
Manufacturers	Durables Manufacturing Exc. Auto	Transportation Equipment Exc. Auto
Manufacturers	Food & Beverage Manufacturing	Beverage and Tobacco Product Manufacturing
Manufacturers	Food & Beverage Manufacturing	Food Manufacturing
Not Elsewhere Classified	Loans to Individuals on Commercial Systems	Private Households
Not Elsewhere Classified	Not Elsewhere Classified (invalid code)	Not Elsewhere Classified (invalid code)
Real Estate	Real Estate & Construction	Heavy and Civil Engineering Construction
Real Estate	Real Estate & Construction	Homebuilding
Real Estate	Real Estate & Construction	Nonresidential Building Contractors
Real Estate	Real Estate & Construction	Real Estate Developer/Owner
Real Estate	Real Estate & Construction	Specialty Trade Contractors
Services	Commercial Services	Administrative and Support Services
Services	Commercial Services	Printing and Related Support Activities
Services	Commercial Services	Waste Management and Remediation Services
Services	Consumer Services	Personal and Laundry Services
Services	Consumer Services	Religious, Grantmaking, Civic, Professional, Similar Orgs
Services	Consumer Services	Repair and Maintenance
Services	Consumer Services	Social Assistance
Services	Entertainment & Recreation	Amusement, Gambling, and Recreation Industries
Services	Entertainment & Recreation	Museums, Historical Sites, and Similar Institutions
Services	Entertainment & Recreation	Performing Arts, Spectator Sports, and Related Industries
Services	Health Care & Pharmaceuticals	Clinics, Labs, Other Services
Services	Health Care & Pharmaceuticals	Doctors/Practitioners
Services	Health Care & Pharmaceuticals	Hospitals
Services	Health Care & Pharmaceuticals	Medical Equipment
Services	Health Care & Pharmaceuticals	Nursing and Residential Care Facilities
Services	Health Care & Pharmaceuticals	Pharmaceutical and Medicine Manufacturing

Sector	Group	Industry
Services	Media & Telecom	Broadcasting (Except Internet)
Services	Media & Telecom	Internet Publishing and Broadcasting
Services	Media & Telecom	ISPs, Web Search Portals, and Data Processing Services
Services	Media & Telecom	Motion Picture and Sound Recording Industries
Services	Media & Telecom	Other Information Services
Services	Media & Telecom	Publishing Industries (Except Internet)
Services	Media & Telecom	Telecommunications
Services	Professional Services	Professional, Scientific, and Technical Services
Services	Restaurant & Hotel	Food Services and Drinking Places
Services	Restaurant & Hotel	Hotels (Accommodation)
Services	Transportation Services	Air Transportation
Services	Transportation Services	Couriers and Messengers
Services	Transportation Services	Rail Transportation
Services	Transportation Services	Scenic and Sightseeing Transportation
Services	Transportation Services	Support Activities for Transportation
Services	Transportation Services	Transit and Ground Passenger Transportation
Services	Transportation Services	Truck Transportation
Services	Transportation Services	Warehousing and Storage
Services	Transportation Services	Water Transportation

Comptroller's Handbook Booklets

"Allowance for Loan and Lease Losses"
"Country Risk Management"
"Loan Portfolio Management"
"Management Information Systems"
"Rating Credit Risk"

OCC Issuances

OCC Bulletin 2001-6, "Expanded Guidance for Subprime Lending Programs" (January 31, 2001)
OCC Bulletin 2006-41, Nontraditional Mortgage Products (NTM), Guidance on NTM Product Risks (October 4, 2006)
OCC Bulletin 2006-46, "Concentrations in Commercial Real Estate Lending, Sound Risk Management Practices: Interagency Guidance on CRE Concentration Risk Management" (December 6, 2006)
OCC Bulletin 2010-16, "Interagency Guidance on Correspondent Concentration Risks" (May 4, 2010)

Other

Basel Committee on Banking Supervision, "Enhancements to the Basel II Framework" (July 2009)
Basel Committee on Banking Supervision, "International Convergence of Capital Measurement and Capital Standards" (June 2006)
High LTV Loans: 12 CFR 34, Subpart D, Appendix A, Supervisory Loan-to-Value Limits

www.ingramcontent.com/pod-product-compliance
Lightning Source LLC
Chambersburg PA
CBHW080743290526
45790CB00008B/3302